HOW TO DRAW
CARS AND TRUCKS
AND OTHER VEHICLES

Michelle Roberts

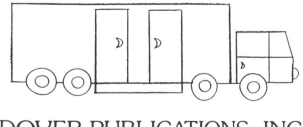

DOVER PUBLICATIONS, INC.
New York

Bibliographical Note

How to Draw Cars and Trucks and Other Vehicles is a new work, first published by Dover Publications, Inc., in 1994.

Library of Congress Cataloging-in-Publication Data

Roberts, Michelle.
    How to draw cars and trucks and other vehicles / Michelle Roberts.
        p.   cm.
    ISBN 0-486-28114-0 (pbk.)
    1. Vehicles in art—Juvenile literature.   2. Drawing—Technique—Juvenile literature. [1. Vehicles in art.   2. Drawing—Technique.]   I. Title.
NC825.V45R63   1994
743′.8962904—dc20   94-16807
                                                                        CIP
                                                                        AC

Manufactured in the United States of America
Dover Publications, Inc., 31 East 2nd Street, Mineola, N.Y. 11501

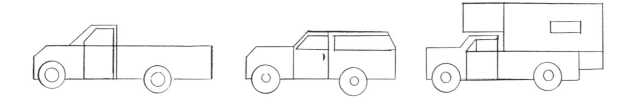

Cars and trucks—and bicycles, trains and planes—are easy to draw. Look at them carefully and you will see that most of them are made up of very simple shapes like rectangles, triangles and circles. All you have to do is draw the shapes and add details like windows and doors. This book has step-by-step diagrams for 28 different vehicles from a sled to a fire engine—and everything in between.

To draw them, just follow the diagrams. Some erasing is called for, so be sure to use a pencil, not a pen. To get you started, let's draw the station wagon shown on page 1. First draw a large rectangle with a smaller rectangle at one end as shown in the top diagram. Draw a slanted line across each top corner of the large rectangle to shape the windshields and across the front top corner of the smaller rectangle to form the hood. Erase the corners as shown by the broken lines. Next add circles for the wheels, erasing the straight lines inside them, and add a vertical line to form the door. Last, add the windows, hubcaps and door handle. All of the vehicles are drawn in the same manner and are just as easy, so have a wonderful time drawing your favorites!

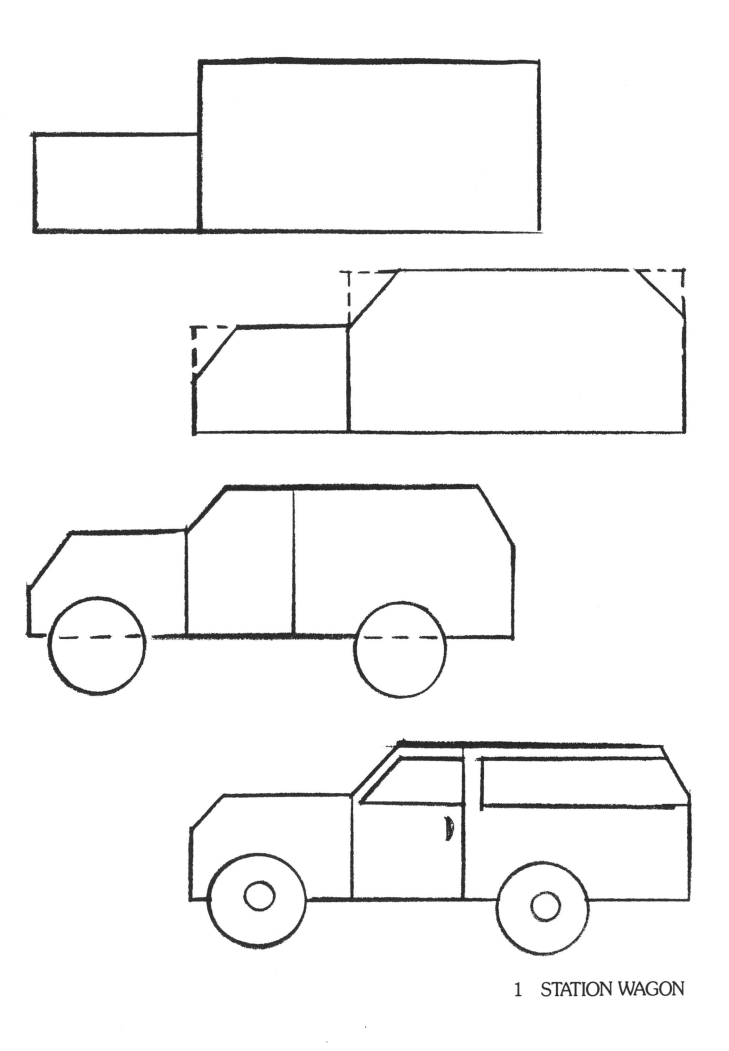

1 STATION WAGON

2   CAR (Side view)

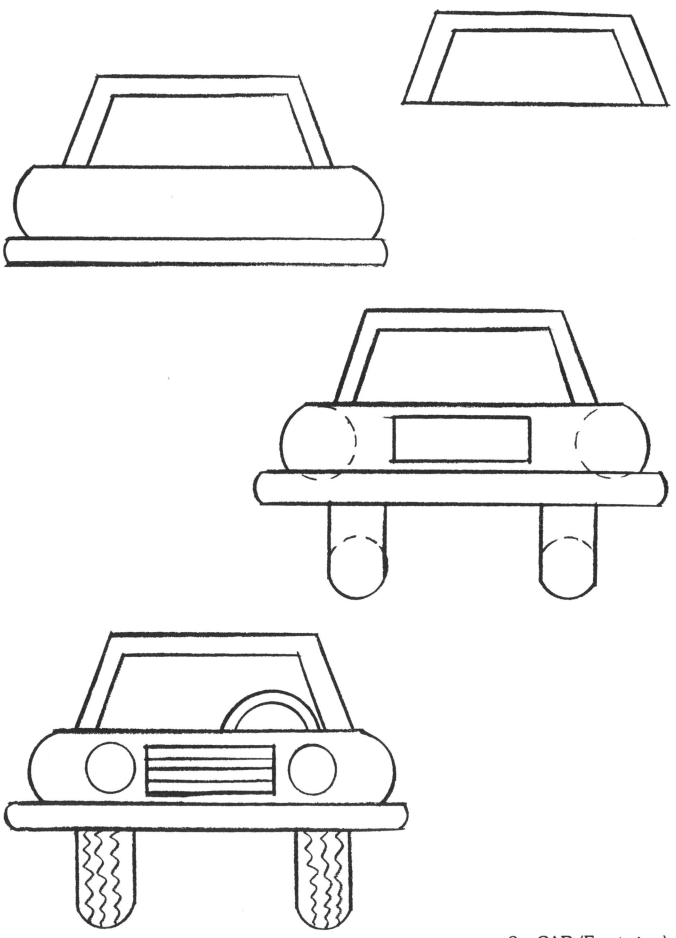

3   CAR (Front view)

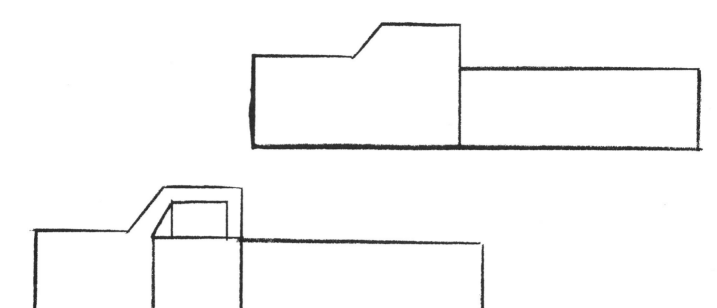

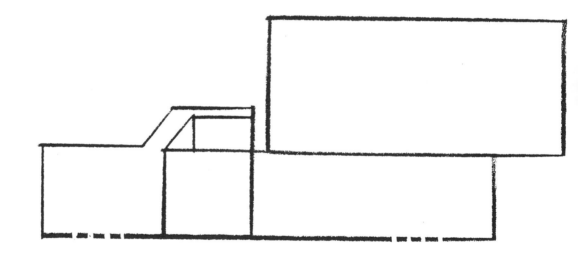

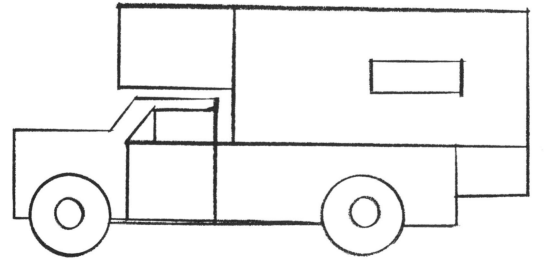

4 CAMPER

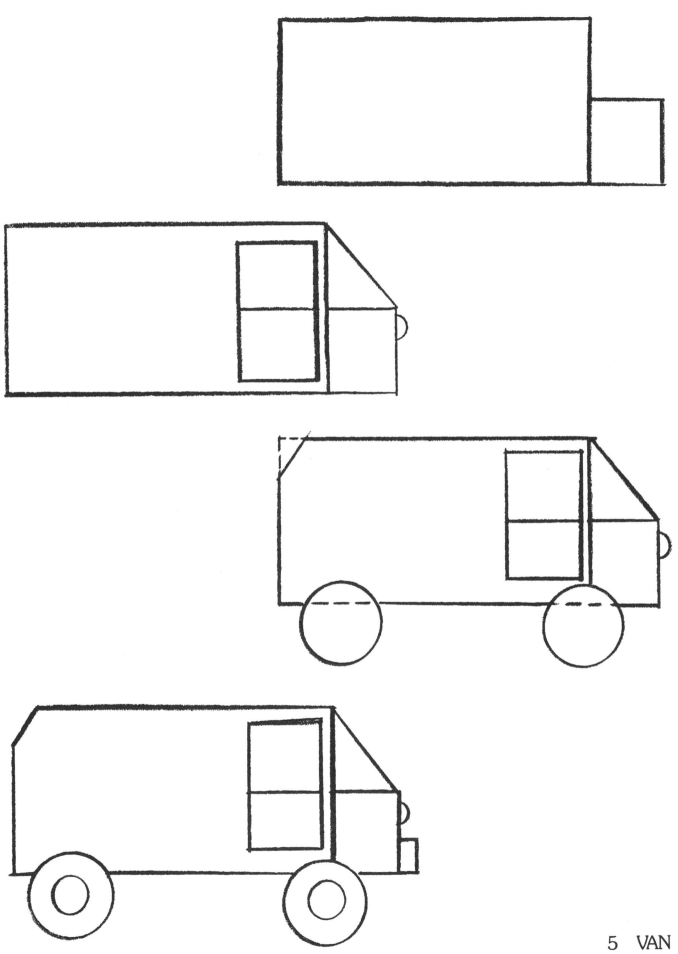

5 VAN

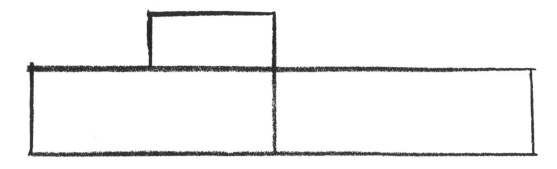

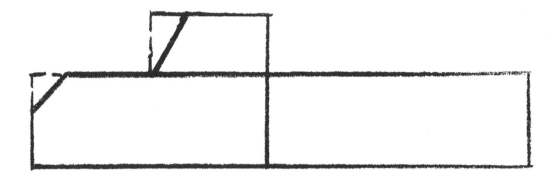

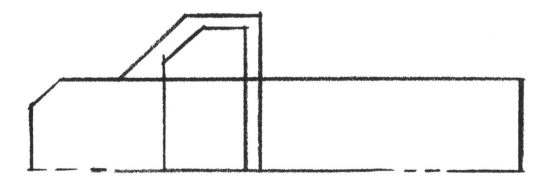

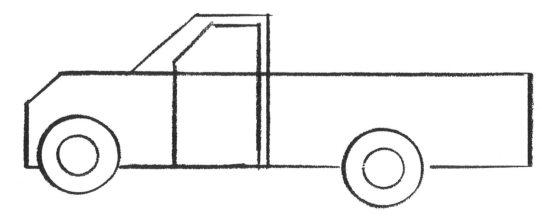

6   PICKUP TRUCK

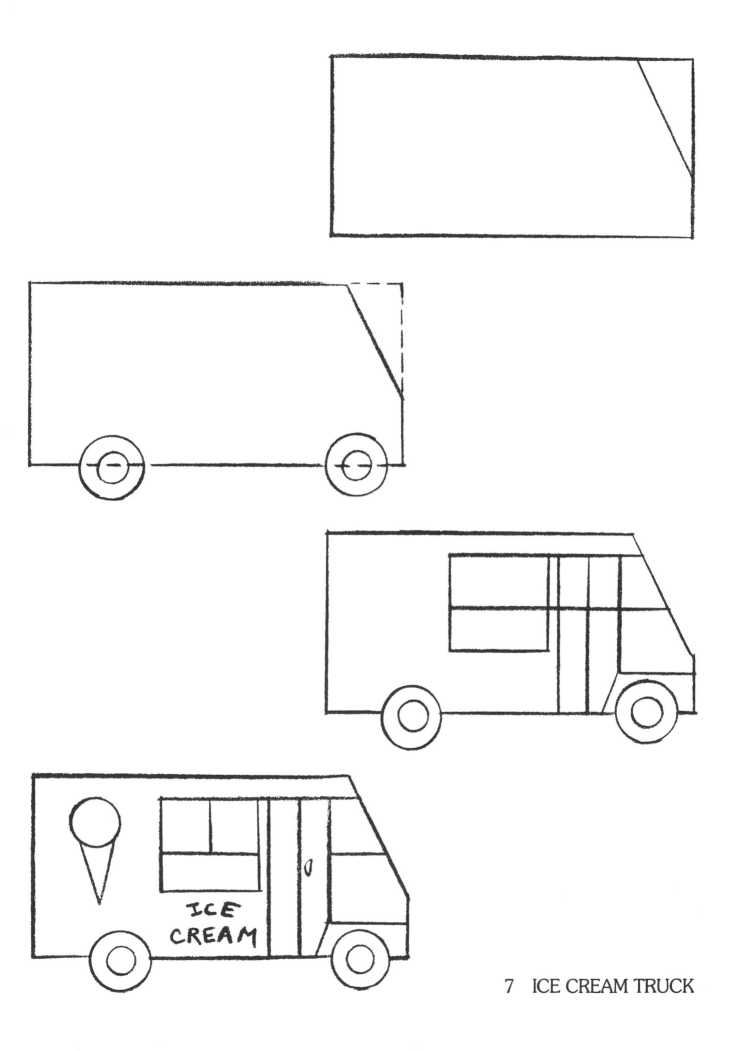

7   ICE CREAM TRUCK

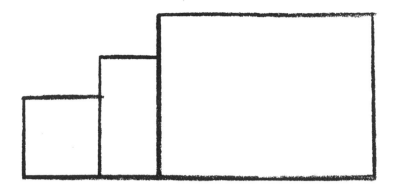

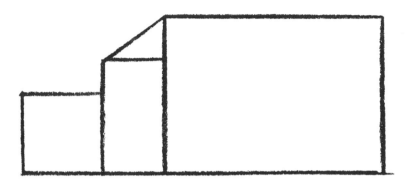

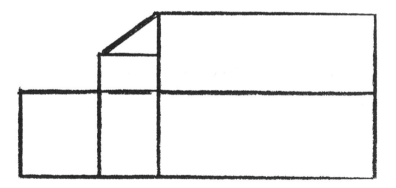

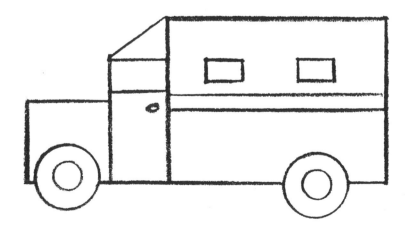

8   ARMORED TRUCK

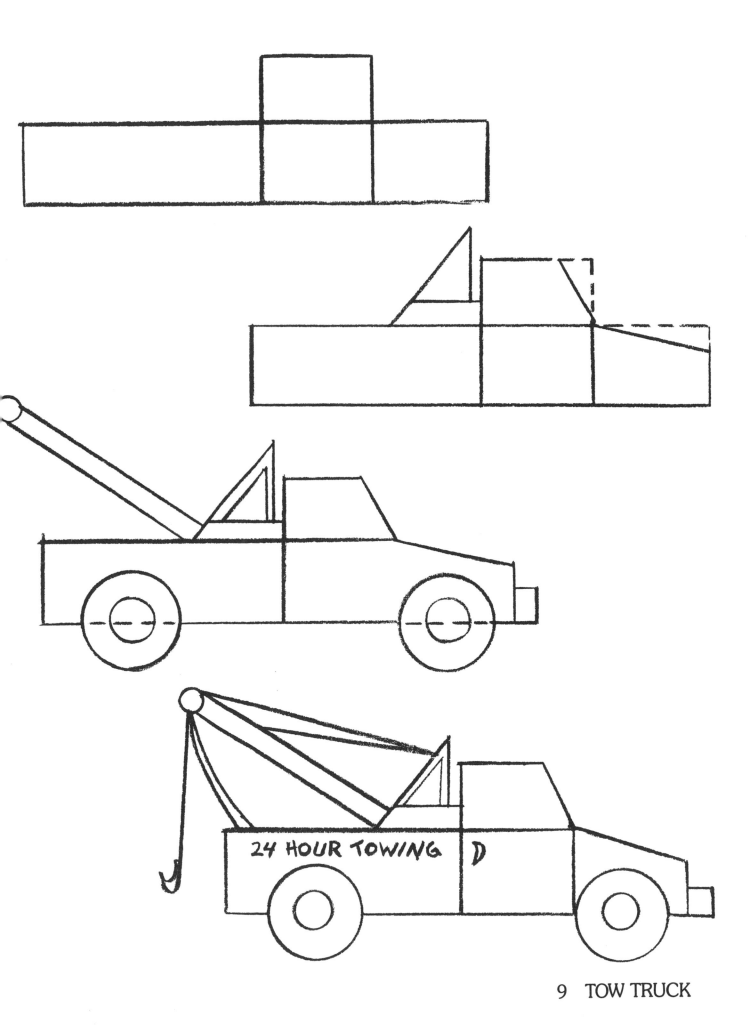

24 HOUR TOWING

9   TOW TRUCK

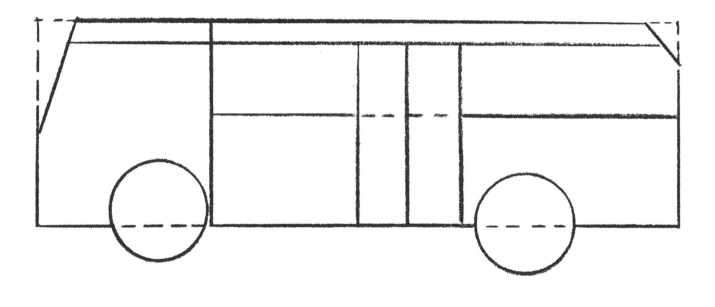

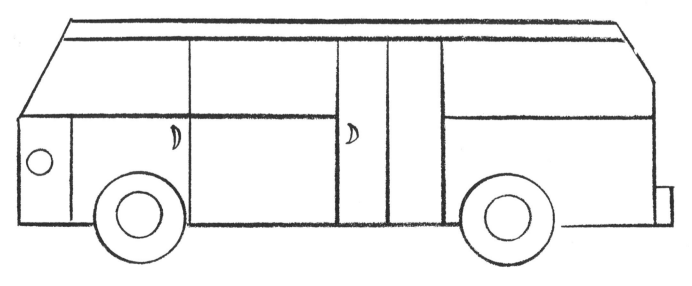

10   BUS

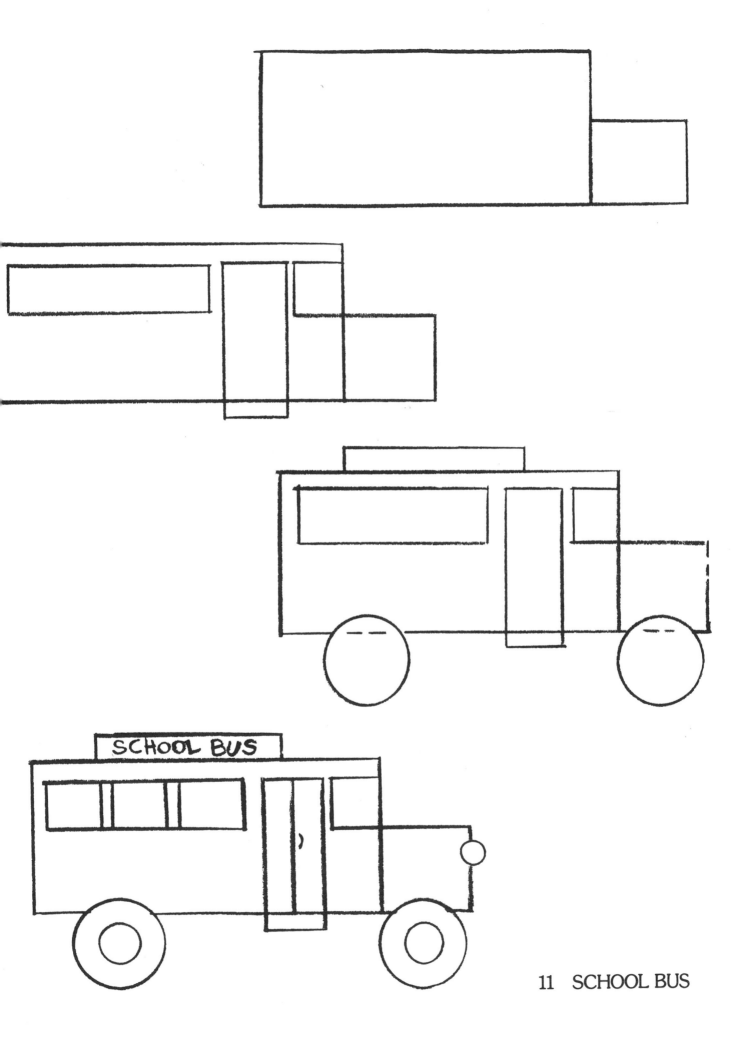

SCHOOL BUS

11   SCHOOL BUS

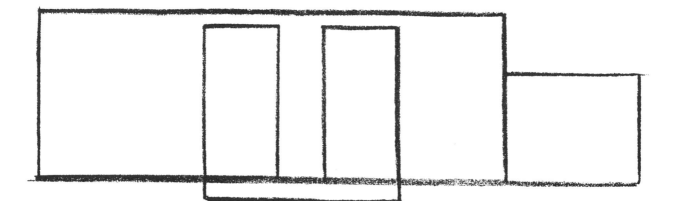

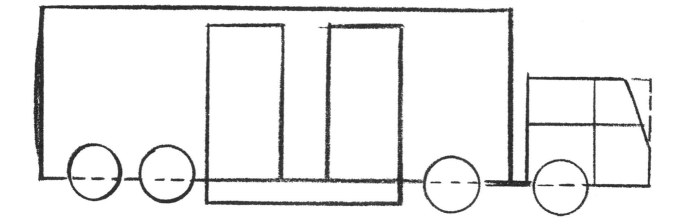

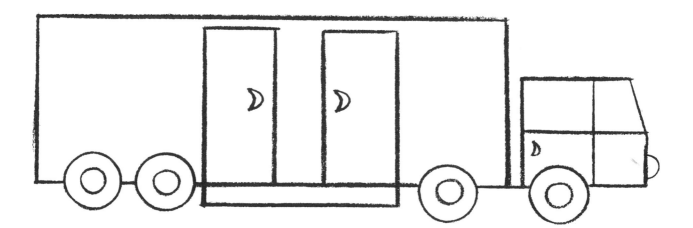

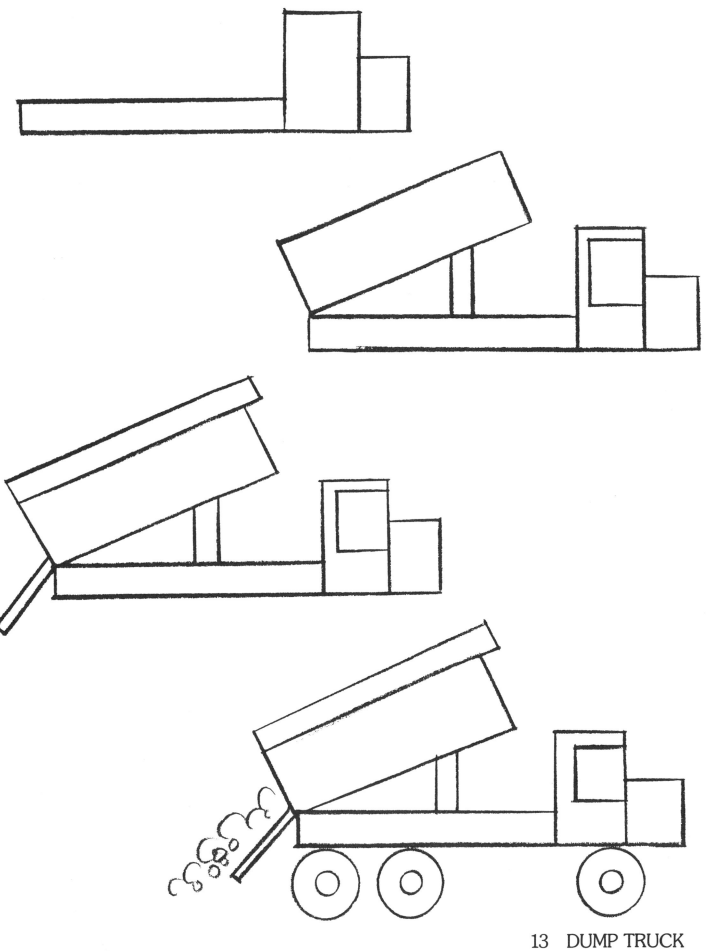

13   DUMP TRUCK

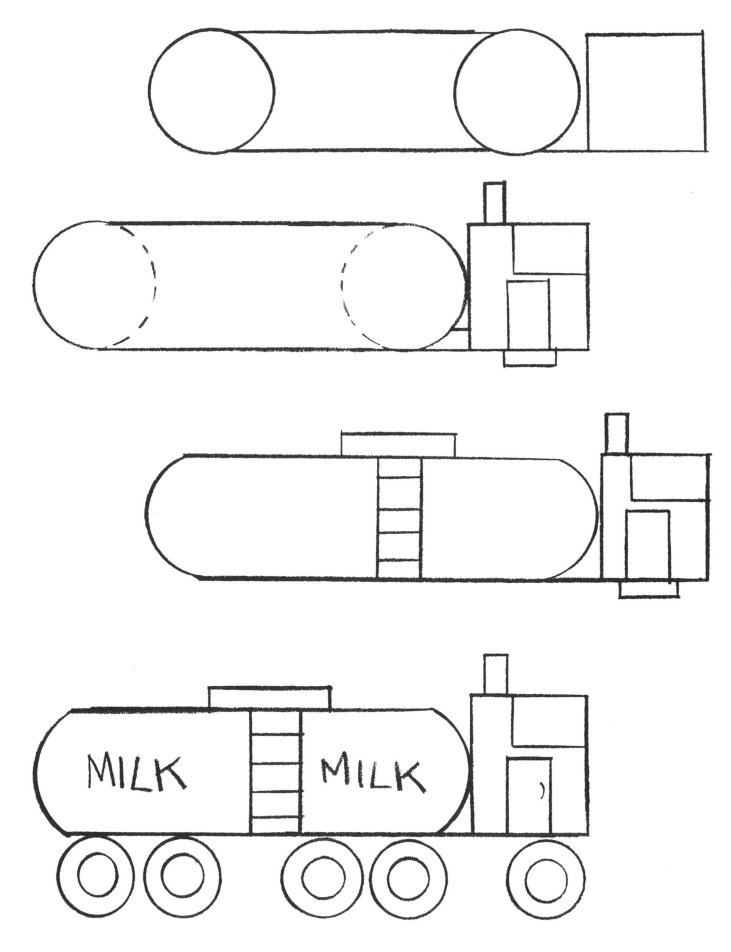

14   MILK TRUCK

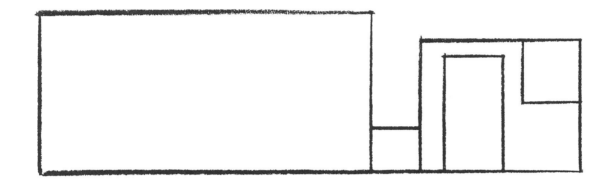

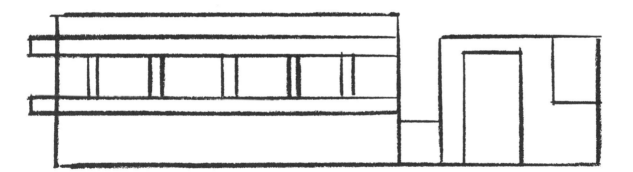

15   FIRE ENGINE

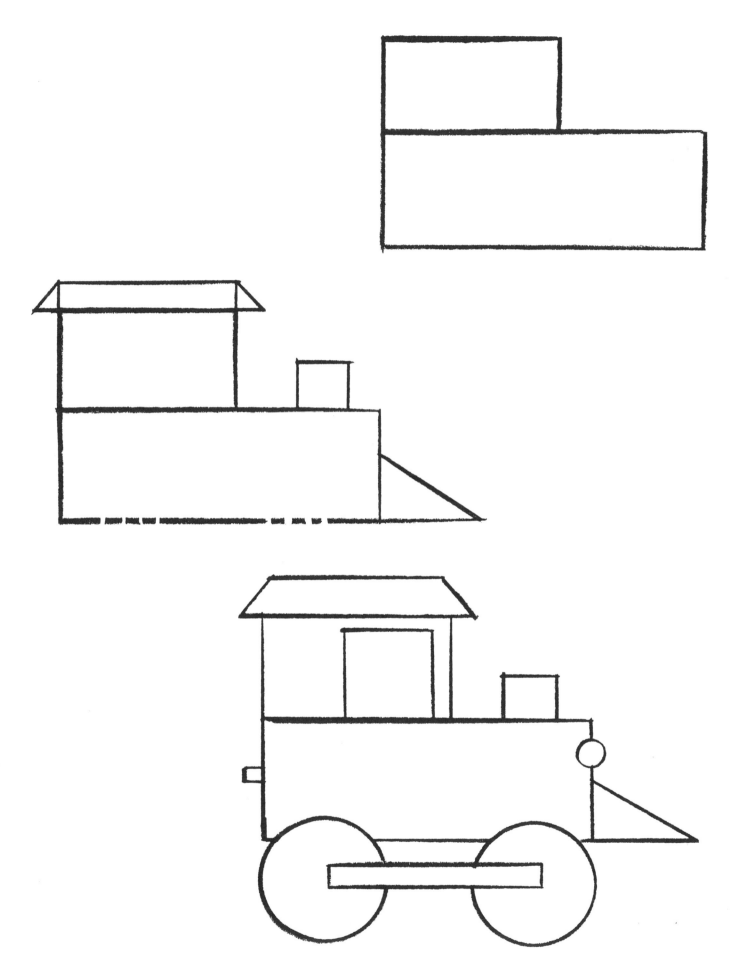

16 LOCOMOTIVE

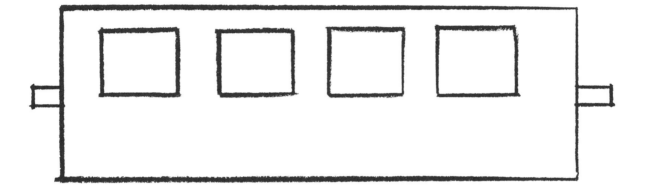

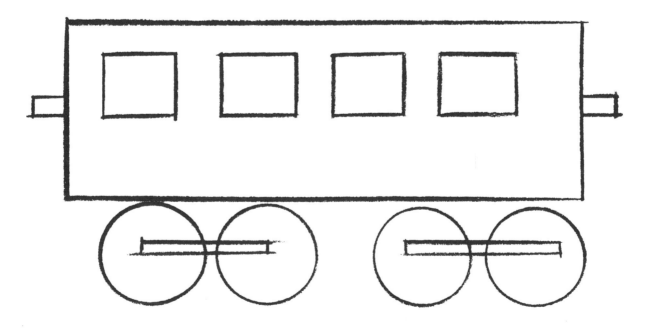

17 RAILWAY COACH/PASSENGER CAR

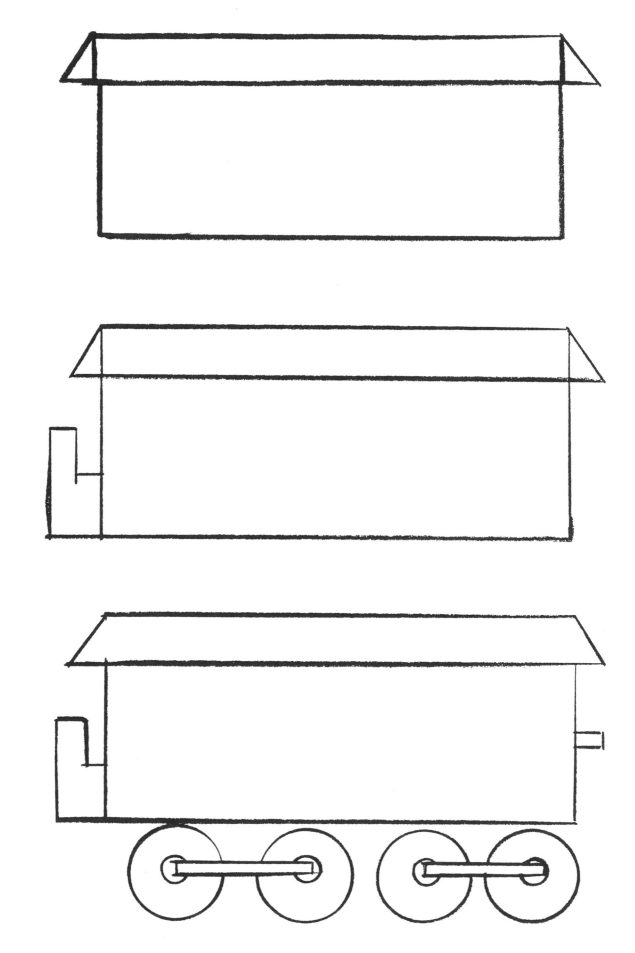

18 CABOOSE

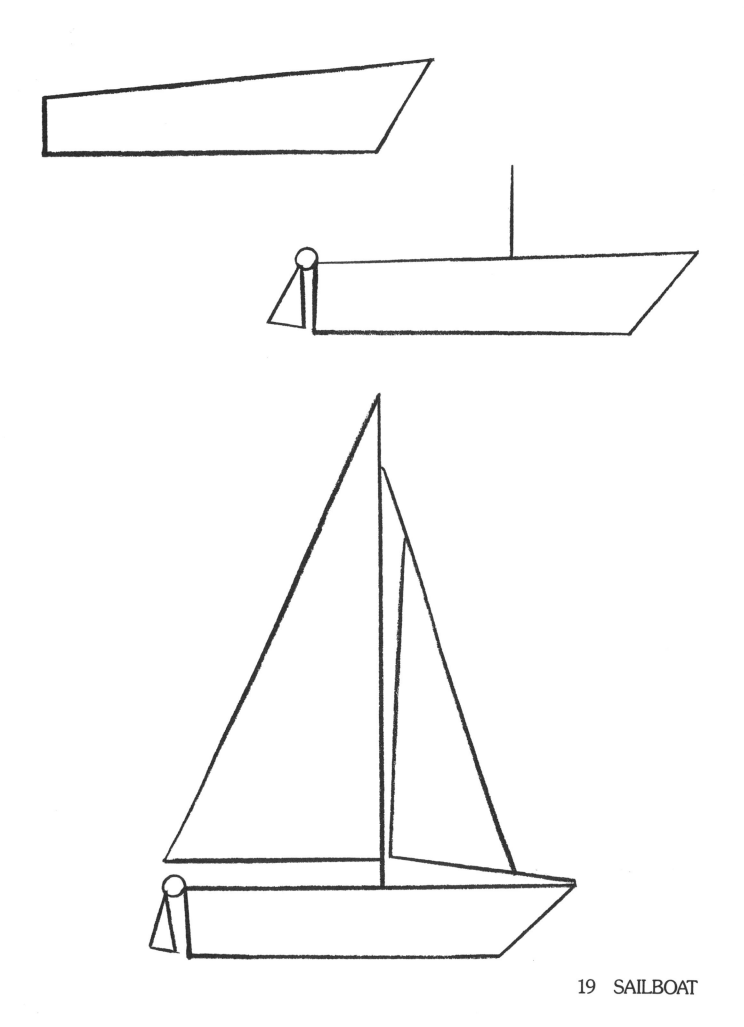

19   SAILBOAT

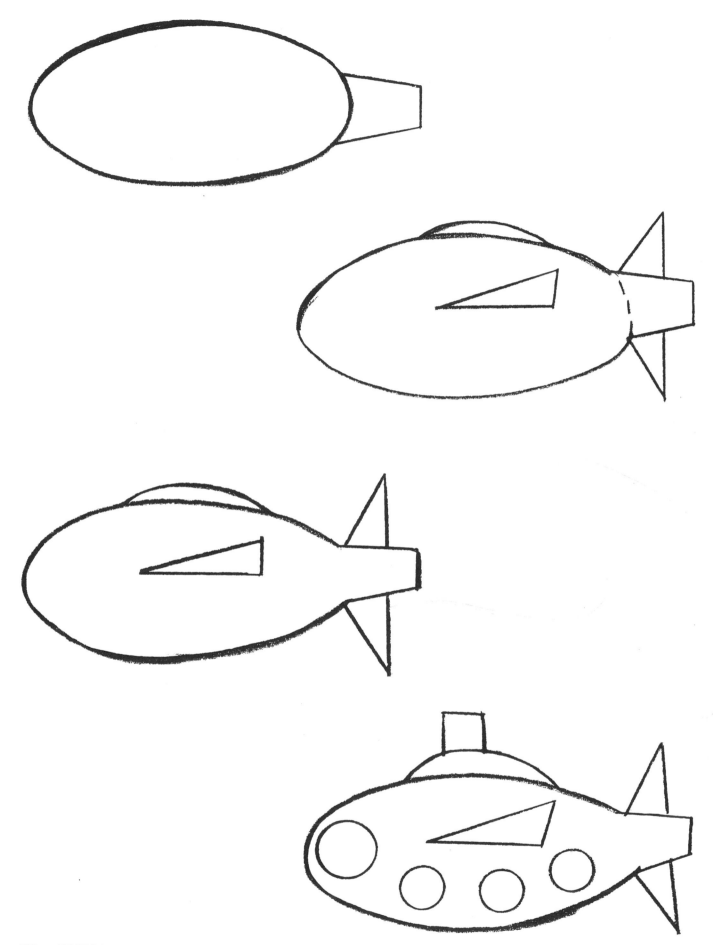

20 SUBMARINE

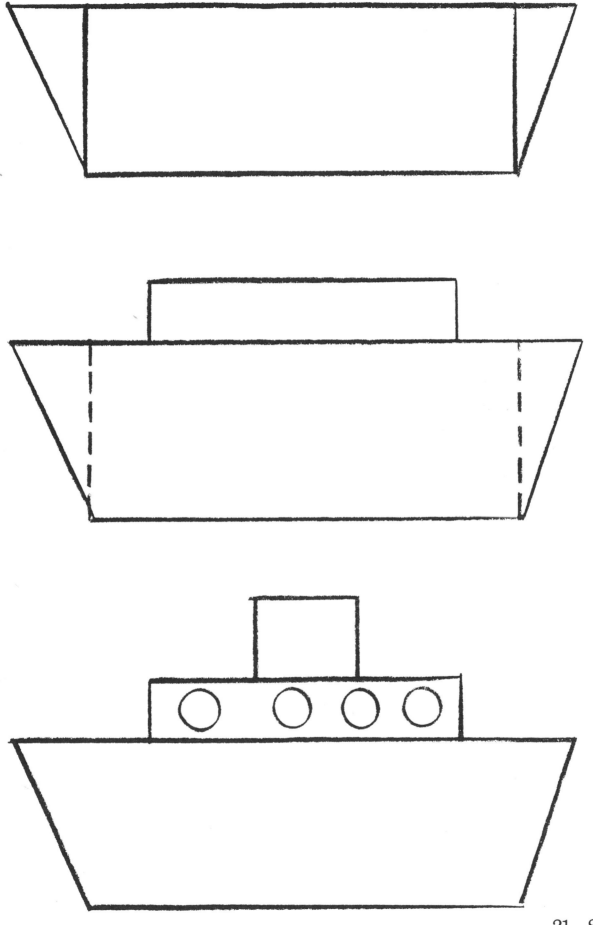

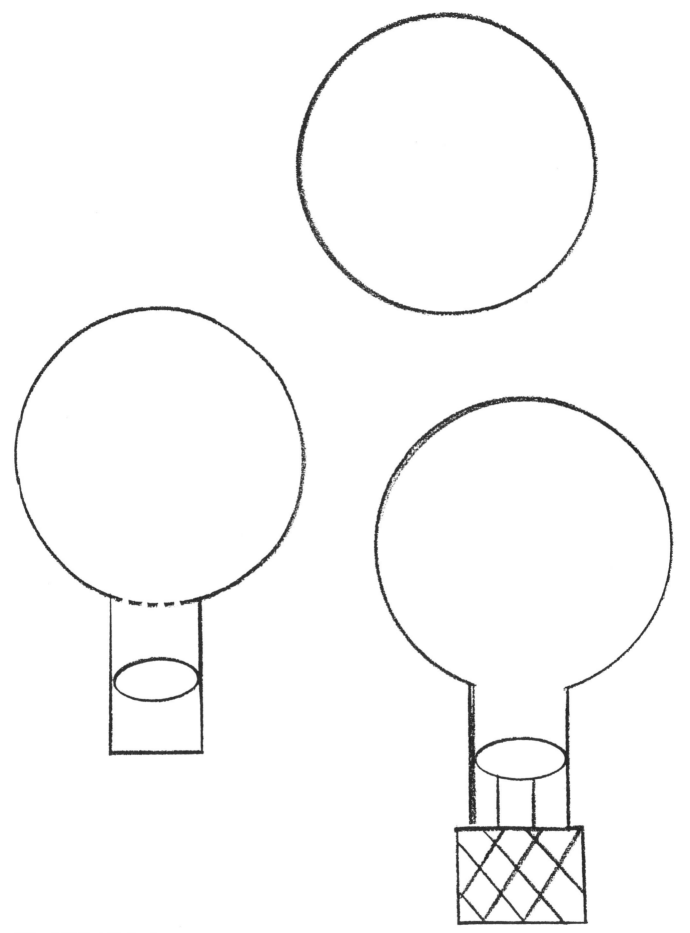

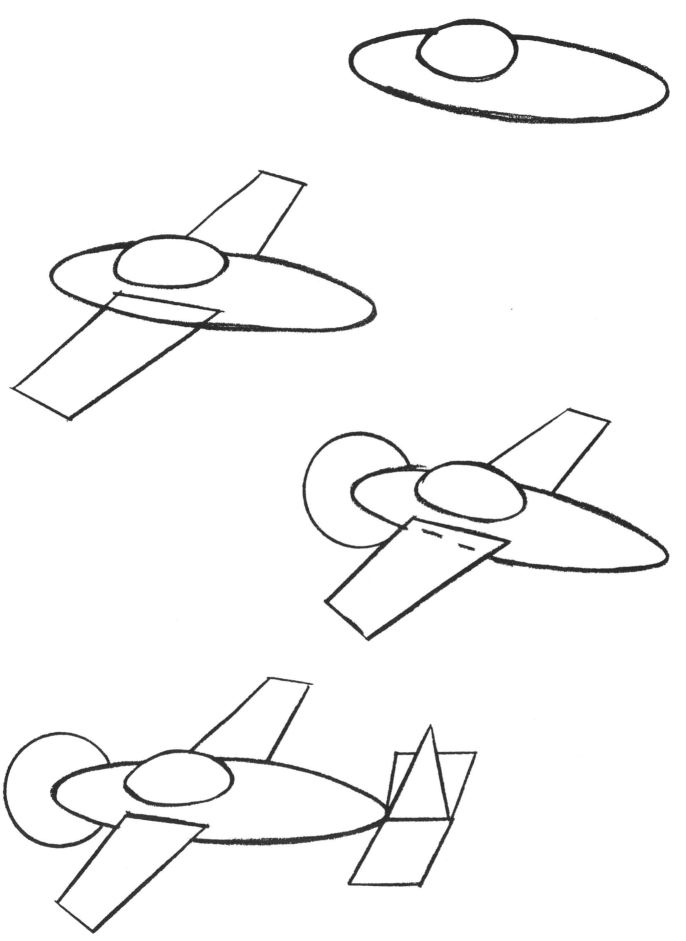

23 AIRPLANE

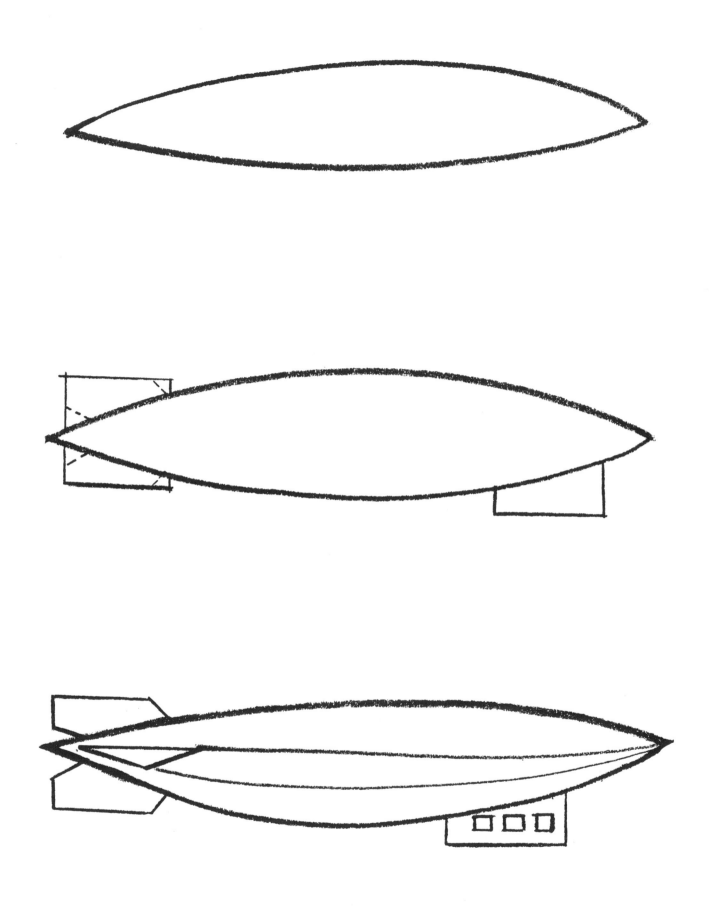

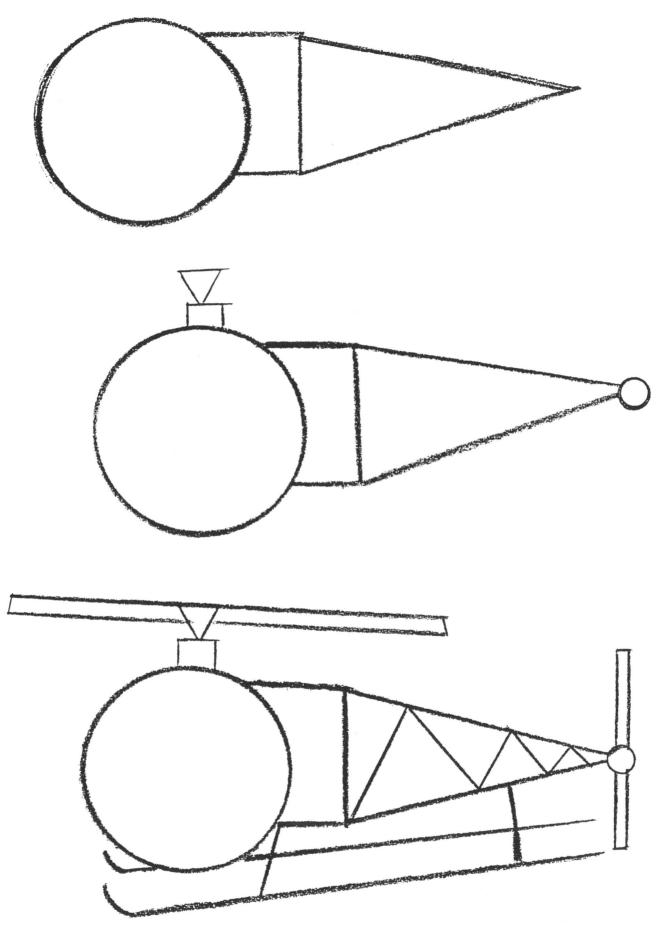

25 HELICOPTER

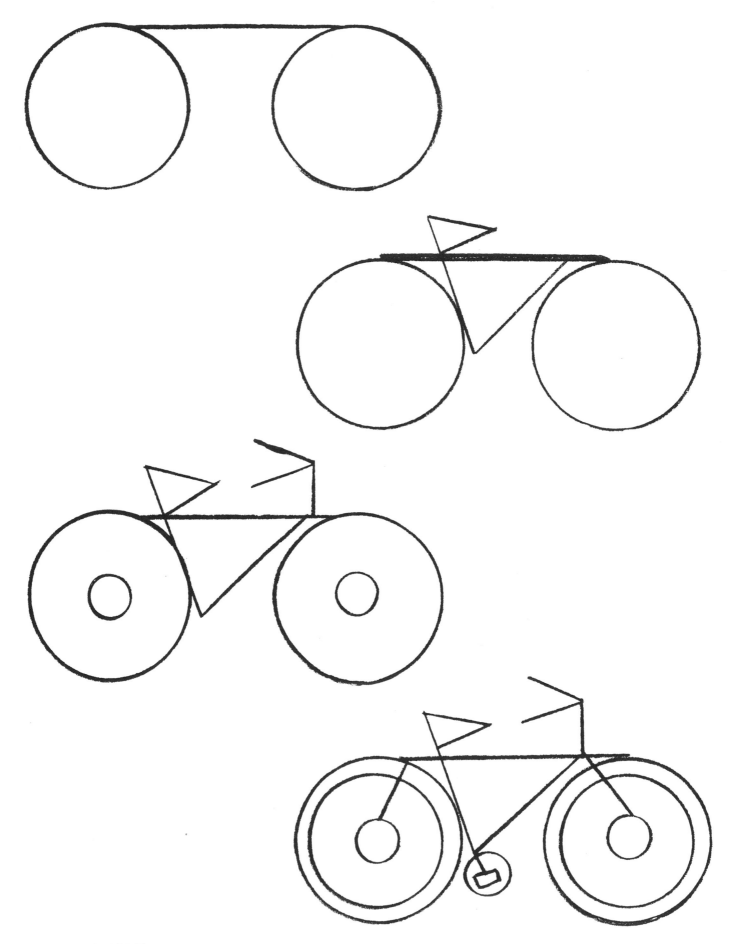

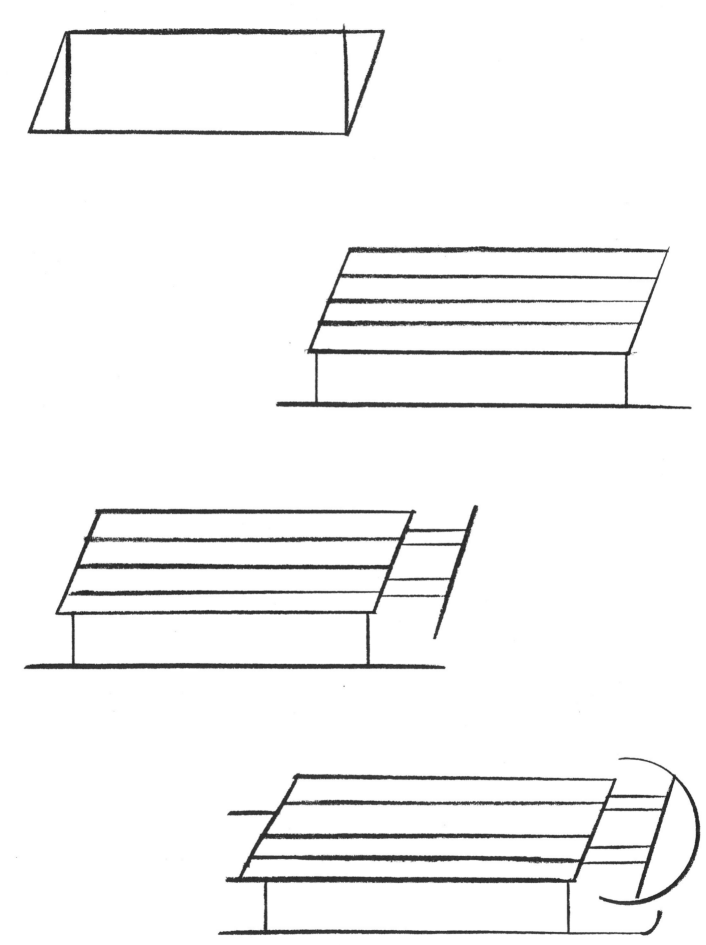